United States Government Accountability Office

Report to the Chairman, Committee on Homeland Security, House of Representatives

I0410733

June 2014

BORDER SECURITY

Opportunities Exist to Strengthen Collaborative Mechanisms along the Southwest Border

June 2014

BORDER SECURITY

Opportunities Exist to Strengthen Collaborative Mechanisms along the Southwest Border

Why GAO Did This Study

According to DHS's CBP, Arizona and South Texas represent some of the highest-threat areas along the southwest border for illegal entrants and smuggling. DHS and CBP coordinate border security with interagency partners, including other federal, state, local, and tribal entities. DHS established collaborative mechanisms in Arizona and South Texas to integrate CBP operations and improve interagency coordination.

GAO was asked to review DHS efforts to coordinate resources along the southwest border. This report (1) describes how DHS uses collaborative mechanisms in Arizona and South Texas to coordinate border security efforts, and (2) examines the extent to which DHS has established performance measures and reporting processes and how, if at all, DHS has assessed and monitored the effectiveness of the collaborative mechanisms in Arizona and South Texas. GAO analyzed documentation, such as campaign plans for the mechanisms; conducted visits to Arizona and South Texas; and interviewed CBP components and interagency partners selected on the basis of agency type and level of participation in the mechanism. Information from these interviews cannot be generalized to all components and partners, but provided insights into the mechanisms.

What GAO Recommends

GAO recommends that CBP assess the JFC and STC, and that DHS, among other things, establish written agreements with ACTT and the STC Unified Command partners. DHS concurred with the recommendations.

View GAO-14-494. For more information, contact Rebecca Gambler at (202) 512-8777 or gamblerr@gao.gov

What GAO Found

The Department of Homeland Security (DHS) has coordinated border security efforts using collaborative mechanisms in Arizona and South Texas, specifically (1) the Joint Field Command (JFC), which has operational control over all U.S. Customs and Border Protection (CBP) resources in Arizona; (2) the Alliance to Combat Transnational Threats (ACTT), which is a multiagency law enforcement partnership in Arizona; and (3) the South Texas Campaign (STC), which integrates CBP resources and facilitates coordination with other homeland security partner agencies. Through these collaborative mechanisms, DHS and CBP have coordinated border security efforts in (1) information sharing, (2) resource targeting and prioritization, and (3) leveraging of assets. For example, to coordinate information sharing, the JFC maintains an operations coordination center and clearinghouse for intelligence information. Through the ACTT, interagency partners work jointly to target individuals and criminal organizations involved in illegal cross-border activity. The STC leverages assets of CBP components and interagency partners by shifting resources to high-threat regions and conducting joint operations.

DHS and CBP have established performance measures and reporting processes for the JFC and ACTT in Arizona and the STC in South Texas; however, opportunities exist to strengthen these collaborative mechanisms by assessing results across the efforts and establishing written agreements. Each collaborative mechanism reports on its results to DHS or CBP leadership through a variety of means, such as accomplishment reports and after-action reports. However, CBP has not assessed the JFC and STC mechanisms to evaluate results across the mechanisms. JFC and STC components GAO interviewed identified challenges with managing resources and sharing best practices across the mechanisms. For example, officials from all five JFC components GAO interviewed highlighted resource management challenges, such as inefficiencies in staff conducting dual reporting on operations to CBP leadership. Best practices for interagency collaboration call for federal agencies engaged in collaborative efforts to create the means to monitor and evaluate their efforts to enable them to identify areas for improvement. An assessment of the JFC and STC could provide CBP with information to better address challenges the mechanisms have faced. In addition, DHS has not established written agreements with partners in the ACTT and STC Unified Command—the entity within STC used for coordinating activities among federal and state agencies—consistent with best practices for sustaining effective collaboration. Officials from 11 of 12 partner agencies GAO interviewed reported coordination challenges related to the ACTT and STC Unified Command, such as limited resource commitments by participating agencies and lack of common objectives. For example, a partner with the ACTT noted that that there have been operations in which partners did not follow through with the resources they had committed during the planning stages. Establishing written agreements could help DHS address coordination challenges, such as limited resource commitments and lack of common objectives.

Contents

Abbreviations

ACTT	Alliance to Combat Transnational Threats
ATF	Bureau of Alcohol, Tobacco, Firearms and Explosives
CBP	U.S. Customs and Border Protection
DHS	Department of Homeland Security
DOI	Department of the Interior
ERO	U.S. Immigration and Customs Enforcement Enforcement and Removal Operations
HSI	U.S. Immigration and Customs Enforcement Homeland Security Investigations
ICE	U.S. Immigration and Customs Enforcement
JFC	Joint Field Command
JOD	Joint Operations Directorate
MOU	memorandum of understanding
OA	Office of Administration
OAM	Office of Air and Marine
OFO	Office of Field Operations
POE	port of entry
STC	South Texas Campaign
TSA	Transportation Security Administration
USDA	U.S. Department of Agriculture

GAO U.S. GOVERNMENT ACCOUNTABILITY OFFICE

441 G St. N.W.
Washington, DC 20548

June 27, 2014

The Honorable Michael T. McCaul
Chairman
Committee on Homeland Security
House of Representatives

Dear Mr. Chairman:

The United States shares over 1,900 miles of border with Mexico, with Arizona and South Texas sharing 387 and 697 miles of that border respectively.[1] The border with Mexico and these two states includes different types of terrain that represent a significant challenge to border security efforts. For example, in Arizona, the border is characterized by desert and rugged mountains, while in South Texas, the border is divided by the Rio Grande. Threats along the southwest border include illegal entrants and the smuggling of drugs, firearms, and currency by criminal networks. According to U.S. Customs and Border Protection (CBP), corridors in Arizona and South Texas represent some of the highest-threat areas along the southwest border for illegal entrants and smuggling.

Securing U.S. borders is the responsibility of the Department of Homeland Security (DHS), in collaboration with other federal, state, local, and tribal entities. CBP, a component within DHS that is the lead agency for border security, is responsible, among other things, for preventing terrorists and their weapons of terrorism from entering the United States and for interdicting persons and contraband crossing the border illegally. Within CBP, the Office of Field Operations (OFO) is responsible for securing the border at ports of entry (POE).[2] The U.S. Border Patrol (Border Patrol) is the CBP component charged with ensuring security along border areas between the POEs. Additionally, CBP's Office of Air and Marine (OAM) provides air and maritime support to secure the

---

[1]South Texas is defined as the region encompassing U.S. Customs and Border Protection's Laredo and Houston Office of Field Operations Field Offices; Del Rio, Laredo, and Rio Grande Valley Border Patrol sectors; and the Del Rio Air Branch, Laredo Air Branch, McAllen Air and Marine Branch, and Houston Air and Marine Branch.

[2]Ports of entry are officially designated places that provide for the arrival at, or departure from, the United States.

GAO-14-494 Border Security

national border between the POEs, within maritime operating areas, and within the nation's interior. DHS and CBP and its components coordinate their border security efforts with various federal, state, local, and tribal entities.

DHS has established collaborative mechanisms throughout the southwest region that are designed to help integrate CBP operations and improve interagency coordination.[3] In September 2013, we reported that DHS has established collaborative mechanisms with both similarities and differences in how they are structured, which missions or threats they focus on, and which agencies participate in them, among other things.[4] In Arizona, CBP realigned its resources in February 2011 through the Joint Field Command (JFC), wherein the operations of all CBP components in Arizona—OFO, Border Patrol, and OAM—report to a single commander. CBP also coordinates with interagency partners in Arizona through the Alliance to Combat Transnational Threats (ACTT), which is a multiagency forum initiated in September 2009 to integrate intelligence and operations among homeland security partners, including DHS's U.S. Immigration and Customs Enforcement (ICE) and the Arizona Department of Public Safety, among others. In South Texas, CBP instituted the South Texas Campaign (STC) in February 2012 to help integrate the activities of CBP components to accomplish specified objectives, such as targeting criminal networks, and to facilitate coordination with homeland security partners, such as ICE and the Drug Enforcement Administration.

You asked us to review how DHS is coordinating resources along the southwest border to achieve an integrated law enforcement response to border security threats. This report addresses the following two questions:

- How does DHS use collaborative mechanisms in Arizona and South Texas to coordinate border security efforts?

---

[3]For the purposes of this review, collaboration is defined as a joint activity by two or more organizations (either within CBP or among CBP and interagency partners) that is intended to produce more public value than could be produced when the organizations act alone. In September 2012, we reported on collaborative mechanisms and the subject matter specialists we interviewed defined an interagency mechanism for collaboration as any arrangement or application that can facilitate collaboration between agencies. See GAO, *Managing for Results: Key Considerations for Implementing Interagency Collaborative Mechanisms*, GAO-12-1022 (Washington, D.C.: Sept. 27, 2012).

[4]GAO, *Department of Homeland Security: Opportunities Exist to Enhance Visibility over Collaborative Field Mechanisms*, GAO-13-734 (Washington, D.C.: Sept. 27, 2013).

- To what extent has DHS established performance measures and reporting processes and how, if at all, does DHS assess and monitor the effectiveness of the collaborative mechanisms in Arizona and South Texas?

To address these objectives, we visited the JFC and the ACTT in Arizona and the STC in South Texas and conducted interviews with officials in CBP headquarters. In Arizona, we visited JFC and ACTT headquarters in Tucson and observed the JFC's Joint Intelligence and Operations Center and an ACTT leadership meeting. We also conducted interviews with JFC and ACTT headquarters officials. In South Texas, we visited STC headquarters in Laredo, where we observed operations at Border Patrol checkpoints and POEs as well as the South Texas Border Intelligence Center, and conducted interviews with STC headquarters officials. During our site visits to Arizona and South Texas, we also met with officials from OFO, Border Patrol, and OAM. Additionally, we conducted semistructured interviews via telephone with officials from 5 CBP component offices from the 21 CBP component locations in Arizona and 5 CBP component offices from the 43 CBP component locations in the South Texas region.[5] We also conducted semistructured interviews via telephone with officials from 6 ACTT partner agencies from the 66 ACTT partner agencies in Arizona and 6 STC Unified Command partner agencies from the 33 STC Unified Command partner agencies in South Texas.[6] We selected component offices to interview based on type of component, the level of threat as defined by the number of CBP apprehensions of illegal entrants, and geographic location. We selected interagency partners to interview based on type of governmental unit and level of participation in the mechanisms. While we cannot generalize information obtained from these interviews to all CBP component offices and interagency partners in

---

[5]We interviewed JFC component officials from the Yuma and Casa Grande Border Patrol Stations, the Nogales and San Luis POEs, and the Tucson Air Branch. We interviewed STC component officials from the McAllen and Laredo South Border Patrol Stations, the Brownsville and Eagle Pass POEs, and the McAllen Air Branch.

[6]The Unified Command is an entity that the STC uses to coordinate with approximately 30 officials from federal, state, and military agencies in South Texas. We interviewed the following ACTT participants: ICE, National Park Service, Arizona National Guard, Arizona Department of Public Safety, Sierra Vista Police Department, and the Tohono O'odham Police Department. We interviewed the following STC Unified Command participants: CBP Rio Grande Valley Border Patrol station; CBP Laredo Field Office; Drug Enforcement Administration (Houston); ICE (San Antonio); Bureau of Alcohol, Tobacco, Firearms and Explosives (San Antonio); and the U.S. Attorney's Office (Laredo).

Arizona and South Texas, information from these interviews provided us with insights into how CBP has coordinated border security efforts.

To describe how DHS uses collaborative mechanisms in Arizona and South Texas to coordinate border security efforts, we reviewed documents from 2009 through 2014 obtained from JFC, ACTT, and STC officials, such as charter documents, establishment memos, and organizational charts, to identify the structure and roles and responsibilities for each mechanism.[7] We also reviewed campaign and operational plans, as well as performance reports, to determine coordination efforts of the mechanisms. To examine the extent to which DHS has established performance measures and reporting processes and how, if at all, DHS has assessed and monitored the effectiveness of the collaborative mechanisms in Arizona and South Texas, we analyzed campaign plans, after-action reports, and accomplishment reports from 2011 through 2014 obtained from the collaborative mechanisms to determine what measures are in place to track outcomes and assess progress.[8] We also conducted interviews with officials from Border Patrol, OFO, and OAM headquarters to determine the extent to which CBP and its components are assessing the benefits and challenges of the JFC, ACTT, and STC. We compared the mechanisms' structures and operations with best practices to enhance and sustain interagency collaboration and *Standards for Internal Control in the Federal*

---

[7]While DHS has established other collaborative mechanisms along the southwest border, our review focused specifically on those mechanisms in Arizona and South Texas—the JFC, ACTT, and STC—as these areas are among the highest-threat areas for illegal entrants and smuggling activity along the southwest border.

[8]We did not evaluate the performance measures; rather we assessed the extent to which the collaborative mechanisms have performance measures in place.

Government.[9] Appendix I presents more details about our objectives, scope, and methodology.

We conducted this performance audit from June 2013 to June 2014 in accordance with generally accepted government auditing standards. Those standards require that we plan and perform the audit to obtain sufficient, appropriate evidence to provide a reasonable basis for our findings and conclusions based on our audit objectives. We believe that the evidence obtained provides a reasonable basis for our findings and conclusions based on our audit objectives.

Background

CBP's three components—OFO, Border Patrol, and OAM—maintain a field structure across the United States and its territories consisting of 20 OFO field offices, 20 Border Patrol sectors, and 3 OAM regions. Within this field structure, each component also manages individual locations; OFO field offices provide oversight of POEs, Border Patrol sectors oversee stations, and OAM regions oversee branches. For example, OAM's Southwest Border Region provides oversight of individual air and marine branches across the southwest border, including locations in both Arizona and South Texas.

As stated in CBP's *Fiscal Year 2009-2014 Strategic Plan*, providing security along the northern, southern, and coastal borders requires effective coordination and integration of all of CBP's operational components, along with the guidance and assistance of essential CBP mission support personnel. One of CBP's objectives is to establish and maintain effective control of air, land, and maritime borders through the use of the appropriate mix of infrastructure, technology, and personnel. To that end, CBP's strategic plan states that gaining and maintaining effective control of the nation's border requires useful intelligence and

---

[9]GAO, *Results-Oriented Government: Practices That Can Help Enhance and Sustain Collaboration among Federal Agencies,* GAO-06-15 (Washington, D.C.: Oct. 21, 2005); GAO-12-1022; and *Standards for Internal Control in the Federal Government,* GAO/AIMD-00-21.3.1 (Washington, D.C.: Nov. 1, 1999). We developed effective practices to enhance and sustain interagency collaboration in GAO-06-15 and GAO-12-1022 by interviewing experts in the area of collaboration and gathering information on select areas where federal agencies have developed substantial ongoing collaborations. These practices are applicable to collaborative mechanisms DHS has established along the southwest border in Arizona and South Texas, as these mechanisms involve interagency collaboration and are intended to help strengthen coordination of border security efforts among participating agencies.

strong partnerships with federal, state, local, tribal, and foreign governments. The JFC, ACTT, and STC are intended to help CBP achieve these objectives, according to CBP documents. For example, the 2011 memo establishing the JFC states that the JFC's responsibility will be to ensure full strategic integration of all CBP assets where feasible and possible in order to maximize operational effectiveness and efficiencies. The ACTT's charter states that the ACTT is to be an effort to maximize the cooperation and coordination of interagency law enforcement efforts in Arizona. Moreover, the STC's establishment memo notes the STC Commander is to serve as the CBP integrator in South Texas, increasing CBP's operational effects through partnerships with stakeholders and communities of interest in South Texas. Figure 1 shows the geographic area that the JFC, ACTT, and STC cover within the southwestern United States.

Figure 1: Geographic Areas of Responsibility of the Joint Field Command (JFC), Alliance to Combat Transnational Threats (ACTT), and South Texas Campaign (STC) along the Southwest Border

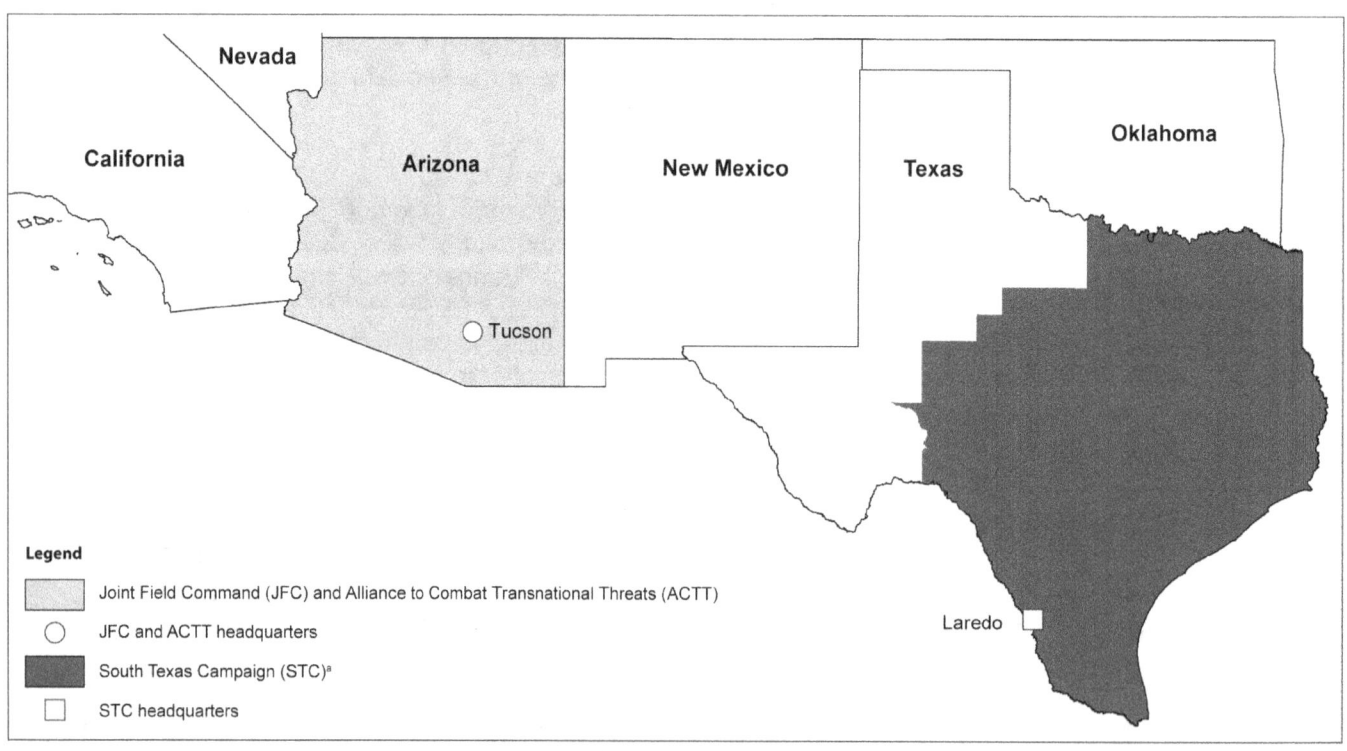

Source: GAO analysis of U.S. Customs and Border Protection information, Mapinfo (map). | GAO-14-494

[a]The STC added the New Orleans Border Patrol sector to the STC in 2013. The New Orleans sector oversees stations in Alabama, Louisiana, and Mississippi.

The three mechanisms have varying structures that aim to integrate CBP operations and improve interagency coordination, as described below.

- **JFC:** The JFC is an entity, under the direction of a commander, with operational control over CBP's resources in Arizona, including OFO, Border Patrol, and OAM resources. Intended to maximize operational effectiveness and efficiencies, the JFC exercises the authority to reallocate staffing and resources among CBP components in Arizona. While the JFC Commander maintains operational control of resources in Arizona, each component's headquarters has authority over administrative decisions for the component, such as providing funding, equipment, and training. The JFC has a dedicated budget of approximately $5 million in fiscal year 2014 that primarily covers personnel costs.
- **ACTT:** The ACTT is a multiagency law enforcement partnership in Arizona designed to address smuggling of aliens, drugs, and bulk cash; exportation of weapons; and hostage taking, among other illegal activities. While it is a DHS initiative, the ACTT concept was implemented by CBP and other federal, state, and local agencies. According to the ACTT Chief of Staff, the ACTT is not under the authority of the JFC; however, the JFC approves CBP-level participation in ACTT operations. The JFC utilizes the ACTT to prioritize tactical targets and coordinate operations with homeland security partners. The ACTT is composed of more than 60 partners representing federal, state, local, military, and tribal organizations.[10] Arizona's ACTT is headed by a 13-member Unified Command, including three JFC component heads, which provides strategic direction to the ACTT as well as guidance for partner interaction. The ACTT does not have a dedicated budget, although CBP components and interagency partners provide funds for administrative, personnel, and operational costs. See appendix II for a full list of ACTT participants.
- **STC:** The STC is an entity that realigned CBP resources, as well as a mechanism for fostering interagency partnerships. As a hybrid of the mechanisms that DHS has in place in Arizona, the STC is intended to enhance coordination both within CBP, as well as with external partners in South Texas. Like the JFC, the STC is managed by a commander; however, the STC Commander exercises less control

---

[10]DHS also maintains a separate ACTT in West Texas/New Mexico, which is not included in the scope of our review.

over the day-to-day operations of CBP components, instead assuming operational control as it specifically relates to the STC mission and objectives, such as conducting targeted operations to disrupt and degrade transnational criminal organizations. As with the JFC, each component's headquarters has authority over administrative decisions, such as providing funding, equipment, and training. The STC Commander coordinates with a Unified Command composed of approximately 30 partners representing federal, state, and military organizations (see app. II for a full list of STC Unified Command participants). While the STC does not have a dedicated budget, the STC has received discretionary funds from the CBP Commissioner's Office, as well as funds from the components, such as resources from Border Patrol targeted for border security efforts in the Rio Grande Valley area.

Table 1 provides additional information on each mechanism, including the staffing, participants, and purpose.

Table 1: Summary of Collaborative Mechanisms in Arizona and South Texas

Mechanism	Staffing	Participants	Purpose
Joint Field Command– Arizona	27 permanent staff members and 35 personnel on temporary detail	U.S. Customs and Border Protection (CBP) components, including the Office of Field Operations (OFO) Tucson Field Office, Office of Border Patrol Tucson and Yuma Sectors, the Office of Air and Marine (OAM) Tucson and Yuma Air Branches and National Air Security Operations Center - Sierra Vista, and the Office of Intelligence and Investigative Liaison	Integrate organizational responsiveness, resource allocation, and decision-making capabilities across Arizona
Alliance to Combat Transnational Threats (ACTT)– Arizona	3 permanent staff members and 19 personnel on temporary detail	CBP; U.S. Immigration and Customs Enforcement (ICE); U.S. Attorney's Office; Bureau of Land Management; U.S. Forest Service; National Park Service; Transportation Security Administration; Arizona Department of Public Safety; Cochise County; Tucson Police Department; Tohono O'odham Nation; U.S. Army; and other federal, state, local, and tribal partners	Leverage the capabilities and resources of partners against individuals and criminal organizations involved in illegal cross-border activity
South Texas Campaign (STC)– South Texas	13 personnel on either permanent or temporary status	STC CBP components, including OFO Laredo and Houston Field Offices; Border Patrol Del Rio, Laredo, Rio Grande Valley, and New Orleans Sectors; and OAM Del Rio Air Branch, Laredo Air Branch, McAllen Air and Marine Branch, and Houston Air and Marine Branch STC Unified Command CBP, ICE, Drug Enforcement Administration, Federal Bureau of Investigation, and other federal and state partners	Integrate intelligence, leverage communities of interest, pursue enhanced coordination with the government of Mexico, and conduct targeted operations to disrupt and degrade transnational criminal organizations

Source: GAO analysis of CBP information. | GAO-14-494

CBP oversees the JFC and the STC through the Joint Operations Directorate (JOD). The JOD was created by the Secretary of Homeland Security in February 2011 and is part of the Office of the CBP Commissioner. The JOD's purpose is to help ensure that CBP-wide missions are being carried out and that CBP maintains a nation-wide focus. Headed by an Executive Director, the JOD is intended to address CBP joint operations coordination, incident management, strategic planning, deliberate planning, and operational doctrine and policy. The JOD is also responsible for defining metrics to determine effectiveness and link CBP strategies to the budget cycle. The JOD is staffed by personnel from CBP components and funding is provided through the Office of the Commissioner. The JOD serves as a liaison for the JFC to Border Patrol, OFO, and OAM headquarters, and the CBP Commissioner for staffing, operations, and other requirements and, according to the JOD Executive Director, plans to serve as a liaison for the STC in the future as well.[11]

DHS Uses Collaborative Mechanisms to Share Information, Target Resources, and Leverage Assets

DHS has taken a number of actions to coordinate border security efforts both within CBP and externally with interagency partners using collaborative mechanisms in Arizona and South Texas in three primary areas: (1) information sharing, (2) resource targeting and prioritization, and (3) leveraging of assets. Coordination efforts have involved sharing of information across geographic areas and organizations, strategic placement of resources to address threats, and the implementation of joint operations, among others.

Information sharing. DHS and CBP have coordinated information sharing among CBP components and participating agencies in the JFC, ACTT, and STC through the development and implementation of various programs or initiatives within these collaborative mechanisms. For example, in Arizona the JFC maintains the Joint Intelligence and Operations Center, which is an operations coordination center and clearinghouse for intelligence information. The Joint Intelligence and Operations Center is staffed by an integrated team of Border Patrol, OFO, and OAM officers and agents that use data, video, and communications systems to coordinate statewide operations. For example, the center monitors real-time air traffic in Arizona and moves air assets where

---

[11]Since the ACTT is a multiagency effort, it is not overseen by CBP.

needed in support of ground operations. In addition, the Joint Intelligence and Operations Center disseminates strategic intelligence to all Arizona field components for immediate action, such as information on targets in Arizona. Among other things, the ACTT initiated focus area meetings in each of five geographic areas of Arizona to allow interagency partners to collaborate and share information related to their specific regions, such as tactics used by drug and alien smugglers, including types of vehicles and common routes.[12] In addition, the ACTT provides intelligence briefings and support to the partners in all of the focus areas. Information sharing in South Texas is facilitated by the South Texas Border Intelligence Center, which the STC created to share intelligence at a centralized location. The South Texas Border Intelligence Center was established to facilitate the sharing and fusion of law enforcement information and intelligence among Border Patrol, OFO, OAM, and interagency partners, such as the Drug Enforcement Administration and the Texas Department of Public Safety. Among other things, the STC has facilitated information sharing between OFO and Border Patrol through OFO sharing knowledge regarding technology used at ports that Border Patrol is leveraging to conduct electronic scans of a larger number of vehicles moving through checkpoints.

Resource targeting and prioritization. DHS and CBP, through the JFC, ACTT, and STC, have established strategies or mechanisms to target and prioritize resources among participating components and interagency partners. For example, in Arizona the JFC created an air integration strategy and a coordinated process of prioritizing and managing air assets through the establishment of an oversight mechanism known as the Air Council. The Air Council sets strategic goals and objectives for the management of all aviation assets in Arizona and meets weekly to set the aviation support air schedule, coordinating with military and other air partners to ensure that geographic areas are prioritized and covered appropriately without the overlap of air assets. In addition, the JFC monitors and analyzes real-time operational data to help target enforcement efforts against transnational criminal organizations. The ACTT is to act as a "force multiplier," as interagency partners can leverage one another's resources and capabilities to target individuals and criminal organizations involved in illegal cross-border activity.

---

[12]CBP defines focus areas as geographic divisions within Arizona that share similar threats, vulnerabilities, and transnational criminal activity levels.

Specifically, partners identify targets based on geographic vulnerabilities and emerging threat information, among other things. The ACTT targets are identified through established focus area meetings and communications between ACTT partner agencies, among other things. In South Texas, the STC jointly selects and prioritizes targets based on intelligence by collaborating with interagency partners through the Unified Command. The STC also established Joint Targeting Teams, which are focused on Unified Command approved targets, which present the highest threats to the area. In addition, the STC formalized an OFO operation that is designed to target transnational criminal organization leaders, members, associates, and family members to cancel their nonimmigrant visas, or place those that have legal permanent resident status in removal proceedings.

Leveraging of assets. DHS and CBP, through the JFC, ACTT, and STC, have leveraged assets of CBP components and interagency partners through resource sharing or joint operations. In Arizona, the JFC established the Canine Council, which integrates OFO and Border Patrol canine resources. In particular, OFO and Border Patrol representatives are to meet on a regular basis to discuss how canines might be used to address threats specific to their geographic areas. For example, Border Patrol canine assets are used at Arizona POEs to cover over 200 shifts per month. The ACTT has leveraged interagency partners' assets by conducting a number of joint operations with interagency partners, including an operation that involved the deployment of increased resources from Border Patrol, the Drug Enforcement Administration, and local law enforcement agencies at a Border Patrol checkpoint and surrounding highways in the western part of Arizona. The operation was designed to disrupt transnational criminal organization activity along the Interstate 10 highway in Arizona. The ACTT also has provided partner agencies with access to resources, such as OAM air support and planning assistance for operations. The STC leverages component and interagency partners' assets in South Texas. For example, the STC shifted Border Patrol assets from Laredo to the Rio Grande Valley in order to augment existing Border Patrol resources and address the current threat environment in the Rio Grande Valley area. Further, the STC conducted joint operations such as an operation that involved assets from multiple Border Patrol stations, OAM, the Department of Defense, the government of Mexico, and the U.S. Attorney's Office. The purpose of the operation was to strategically place resources at and between POEs in South Texas in order to increase border security.

DHS Has Established Performance Measures and Reporting Processes for the JFC, ACTT, and STC, but Could Strengthen These Collaborative Mechanisms

DHS and CBP Have Performance Measures and Reporting Processes in Place for Collaborative Mechanisms in Arizona and South Texas

DHS and CBP have established processes, including objectives and performance measures, to report on the results of the JFC, ACTT, and STC, and these reporting processes vary across the mechanisms. For example, the STC develops and reports on specific quantitative performance measures for operations, while the JFC and the ACTT use and report on a mix of quantitative and qualitative measures to assess their activities. Some of the quantitative performance measures developed by the JFC, ACTT, and STC are existing metrics used by CBP and its components to assess and report on progress of their specific border security activities. For example, the ACTT reports on seizures of narcotics and currency as performance measures to assess efforts to disrupt, degrade, and dismantle criminal organizations operating in Arizona. CBP established these measures to assess and report on border security efforts. Further, the STC reports on apprehensions of illegal entrants as a performance measure to assess the success of various operations. This measure was established by Border Patrol to assess and report on its enforcement efforts between POEs. The objectives and performance measures reported by each collaborative mechanism are summarized in table 2.

Table 2: Summary of Objectives and Performance Measures Reported by the Collaborative Mechanisms

Mechanism	Objectives	Performance measures
Joint Field Command (JFC)– Arizona	The JFC is focused on all U.S. Customs and Border Protection (CBP) objectives in Arizona, specifically: • manage the border • expedite lawful trade and travel • manage risk • integrate missions	The JFC has performance measures in place across areas such as conducting targeted actions to mitigate risk posed by transnational criminal organizations and implementing innovative solutions to promote border security. The performance measures are a mix of quantitative and qualitative measures and include reducing illicit cross-border activity, developing and implementing new strategies to combat border security threats, and improving air and ground coordination.
Alliance to Combat Transnational Threats (ACTT)– Arizona	• Identify, prioritize and execute actions against common threats and targets in each focus area • Conduct sustained and unified actions against prioritized threats in each focus area • Enhance the level of collaboration, principally in the areas of interagency participation, transparency, and information sharing • Leverage intelligence, investigations, and interdiction to disrupt threats in Arizona • Enhance situational awareness in order to more effectively detect, identify, classify, and track threats • Enhance the ability to respond to and resolve identified threats	The ACTT maintains performance measures across the mechanism's four objectives. Performance measures are both quantitative and qualitative, including initial increases in narcotics, currency, and weapons seizures; increased arrests and prosecutions of criminal organizations' personnel; increased citizen calls reporting activity; and changes in concealment methods at ports of entry.
South Texas Campaign (STC)– South Texas	• Integrate intelligence, analysis, and targeting throughout the South Texas region • Engage communities of interest in order to degrade transnational criminal organizations' ability to operate throughout the region's communities • Engage, sustain, and enhance bi-national efforts with the government of Mexico in order to degrade the critical capabilities of transnational criminal organizations within the region and the adjoining states of Mexico • Incorporate a flexible, mobile, and unified South Texas region workforce to address emerging threats • Disrupt and degrade transnational criminal organizations' ability to use established air, land, and sea routes of egress and ingress	The STC develops specific goals, objectives, metrics, and performance indicators for each operation. The metrics and performance indicators are designed to allow operational planners to categorize, evaluate, predict, and improve STC operations. Metrics and performance indicators vary based on the operation and can include increases in apprehensions; decreases in the number of illegal entries; changes in the recidivism rate; and changes in tactics, techniques, and procedures of transnational criminal organization in the area. The STC is to reevaluate the metrics and performance indicators on a regular basis to ensure that they are aligned with operational strategies.

Source: GAO analysis of CBP information. | GAO-14-494

The type and frequency of reporting varies by each collaborative mechanism. Each collaborative mechanism reports on its results to its leaders, or DHS or CBP leadership, through a variety of means, such as accomplishment reports and after-action reports, as discussed below.

- **JFC.** The JFC reports on its results through quarterly progress reports, an initial accomplishment report, and operational after-action reports. First, the JFC develops quarterly progress reports, which are to be reviewed by JFC leadership. The quarterly progress reports began in fiscal year 2014 and provide information on new threats, high-traffic areas, and available resources. JFC leadership reviews the reports to assess progress made toward the JFC's objectives and to determine whether changes are needed to JFC priorities based on changes to threats or border security activities identified in the report, according to JFC officials. Second, the JFC developed a report providing information on its initial accomplishments from its establishment in 2011 through 2013. This report provided information on JFC accomplishments in the areas of integrated operations and planning, sharing of information and skills among components, joint intelligence gathering, military coordination, and integrated resources. Finally, the JFC is to prepare after-action reports for each operation. These after-action reports provide information on the operation's mission, use of resources, and operational results. For example, in an operation from October 2012 through July 2013, the JFC reported the following statistics from sustained outbound inspections: approximately $5.3 million in seized currency and 881 arrests.[13] The JFC uses these after-action reports to debrief operations and to provide comments and recommendations for future operations. JFC and component leadership also discuss results of operations during biweekly teleconferences, according to JFC documents.
- **ACTT.** The ACTT reports information on its results through annual accomplishment reports; periodic, ad hoc reports; and after-action reports. For example, the ACTT produces annual accomplishment reports to report its results. In these accomplishment reports, the ACTT reports information on operations, tactics employed, intelligence, trends, and partner activities. The ACTT also reports on its results to DHS, CBP, and ICE leadership on an ad hoc basis upon request. For example, CBP has periodically requested ACTT progress reports on such things as the number of joint operations completed and their results, in connection with its year-end accomplishment reporting. In addition, the ACTT is to prepare after-action reports for each of its operations. These after-action reports contain information intended to help ACTT leadership determine whether the ACTT

---

[13]Outbound inspections involve the screening of vehicles and persons leaving the United States in order to stem the outbound flow of currency and fugitives from the country.

should engage in additional phases of an operation. For example, a joint operation of Border Patrol and ICE, under the auspices of the ACTT, during November 2013, reported 34 arrests, 381 pounds of marijuana seized, and 1 recovered stolen vehicle.

- **STC.** The STC reports on its results through annual, weekly, and after-action reports. Specifically, the STC reports on its results through an annual accountability report provided to CBP headquarters. These annual accountability reports provide information on the STC's progress toward meeting operational and administrative milestones, accomplishments related to each of the STC's five objectives, and best practices across the South Texas region. Reported accomplishments in the fiscal year 2013 accomplishment report include intelligence sharing among interagency partners to identify targets and the completion of several joint operations. The report also includes performance measures for several operations, such as the number of arrests and seizures of drugs and currency. Across the South Texas region, the STC reported the disruption and degradation of the capabilities of transnational criminal organizations through the arrest of 231 approved targets. Beginning in fiscal year 2014, the STC also prepares weekly status reports for Unified Command members and CBP headquarters, which include information on coordination efforts with other agencies as well as updates on operations. Additionally, the STC prepares an after-action report for each operation. For example, in an operation from June through September 2013, under the auspices of the STC, the Rio Grande Valley sector reported making 2,756 apprehensions of illegal entrants and seizing approximately 4,585 kilograms of marijuana. During the same operation, the Laredo sector reported making 223 apprehensions of illegal entrants and seizing 4,085 kilograms of marijuana. According to STC officials, they use after-action reports to confirm whether the operation achieved the anticipated results and to determine if new strategies are necessary for future operations. The STC uses information in after-action reports to brief the STC Unified Command at quarterly meetings and provide ad hoc updates to the CBP Commissioner.

According to a senior JOD official, the JOD is working with components to standardize reporting processes among the JFC, STC, and ACTT. According to the official, the JOD envisions obtaining regular (e.g., biweekly) reports from each mechanism regarding progress made toward achieving its annual objectives. The intent of these reports, once implemented, will be to help ensure that CBP's collaboration with other agencies is carrying out CBP's mission.

Assessment of Collaborative Mechanisms, Written Agreements, and a Monitoring Mechanism Could Strengthen Integration and Coordination Efforts along the Southwest Border

Opportunities exist to strengthen collaborative mechanisms by conducting an assessment of results across the mechanisms and establishing written agreements and a strategic-level mechanism to monitor coordination efforts. Specifically, DHS has not assessed the JFC and STC mechanisms to determine their relative benefits and challenges. Moreover, DHS has not established written agreements or a monitoring mechanism that could help facilitate and strengthen coordination with interagency partners in the ACTT and the STC Unified Command.

DHS Could Benefit from an Assessment of the JFC and STC Mechanisms

CBP has not assessed the JFC and STC to evaluate results across the mechanisms to identify any possible areas for improvement. Our analysis of CBP documentation on the JFC and STC as well as our interviews with headquarters and field officials identified two primary challenges experienced by the JFC and STC: (1) resource management challenges and (2) limited sharing of best practices across mechanisms. An assessment of the JFC and STC mechanisms could provide CBP with information to help better address these challenges.

Resource management challenges. JFC and STC component officials reported to us resource management challenges that, while different in nature, could be evaluated through an assessment of these mechanisms. The Fiscal Year 2013 JFC Campaign Plan states that the JFC mission is to integrate organizational responsiveness, resource allocation, and decision-making capabilities to improve efficiencies and effectiveness; however, our interviews with officials from all five JFC components highlighted resource management challenges with the JFC. For example, the JFC Chief of Staff stated that Border Patrol canine teams have been successfully used at POEs in Arizona for a number of years and that Border Patrol station and OFO port leadership jointly determine canine requirements and priorities and address any gaps in coverage and operational needs with their combined canine assets. In addition, the JFC Chief of Staff stated that Border Patrol and OFO canines are routinely used at POEs and can be interchanged between CBP components in many environments. The Chief of Staff noted that the deployment of Border Patrol canine teams to POEs serves as a force multiplier. However, some officials we interviewed provided different perspectives on the use of canines. For example, three JFC component officials in Arizona we interviewed cited challenges, from their perspective, in how the JFC has used Border Patrol and OFO canine resources. For example, these officials in Arizona told us that the JFC has attempted to integrate the canine resources of Border Patrol and OFO by reassigning canines from Border Patrol stations to POEs; however, they stated that, in their view, the reassignment of canines can contribute to inefficiencies because, among other things, Border Patrol canines are not used to working in the POE environment. CBP headquarters officials from both OFO and Border Patrol stated that canines are not easily interchanged between CBP components. Specifically, according to OFO officials, Border Patrol canines have less frequent contact with passengers, do not receive training on searching pedestrians, and can be more aggressive than OFO canines, which are used to working closely with passengers entering and leaving the United States. According to a Border Patrol headquarters official, in his view, the JFC has shifted canines from higher-threat areas along the border to a lower-threat POE, despite the fact that the port is not an area priority and receives a nominal amount of traffic.

Moreover, CBP component officials stated that dual reporting on JFC activities can contribute to inefficiencies in the use of resources and could result in duplication of effort. In its initial accomplishment report, the JFC notes as a success the consolidation of reporting through the Joint Intelligence and Operations Center to provide CBP field and headquarters' leadership with a single source for all Arizona operational reporting. However, our interviews with officials from all five CBP components identified challenges in the reporting of information from the field to headquarters units. For example, according to JFC officials, all JFC components—OFO, Border Patrol, and OAM—are required to report operational matters, such as significant incidents involving the use of weapons, through the Joint Intelligence and Operations Center to the CBP Commissioner's office. However, according to CBP component officials, the heads of OFO, Border Patrol, and OAM have identified a need to receive the same information on these operational matters. Thus, OFO, Border Patrol, and OAM officials in Arizona typically report information to both the JFC and their own chains of command in their own components, resulting in dual reporting. In addition, CBP component officials in Arizona stated that it can be challenging reporting port-related information to the JFC because JFC staff members may not have knowledge of port operations. For example, a senior OFO official stated that the JFC has directed a significant amount of follow-up questions to a POE on the data it reported because Border Patrol agents handle the JFC reporting process, and these Border Patrol agents do not have familiarity with port operations, which can create a burden for the components.

In addition, officials we interviewed stated that the STC has experienced resource challenges related to limited funding and personnel. The STC has no permanent staff and depends on a rotation of personnel from CBP components (e.g., Border Patrol, OFO, OAM) through the STC, as additional positions were not created to support the STC. Four of five CBP component officials we interviewed stated that limited resources are an overall challenge of the STC, and three of these component officials noted that detailing personnel to the STC can create staffing challenges. An official from one Border Patrol station in South Texas stated that the STC is pulling top resources from the station and that this creates challenges with backfilling the positions at the station and training the new staff. OFO officials also told us that POEs in South Texas have limited personnel to conduct port operations, making it difficult for POEs to provide personnel resources to the STC. In January 2013, the STC completed a staffing forecast, projecting ongoing staffing and resource needs that discusses the STC's dependence on components to provide staff and resources to support the STC. The staffing forecast noted that this practice is not sustainable. According to senior STC headquarters officials, CBP headquarters has not taken any action on the STC's staffing forecast because of staff turnover. An assessment of the JFC and STC could help CBP better understand areas for possible improvement related to resource management, such as the resources needed to implement these mechanisms and how to use the mechanisms' resources efficiently.

Limited sharing of best practices across mechanisms. Opportunities also exist for CBP components to share best practices across Arizona and South Texas. The CBP Commissioner's fiscal year 2014 operational priorities state that CBP should take the best practices of existing innovative and successful initiatives and apply them agency-wide. Further, both the STC Campaign Plan and the JFC Commander's intent state that the mechanisms should capture and replicate best practices to better fulfill their missions and improve strategies; however, CBP has not assessed the potential application of best practices across these mechanisms. The JFC has shared some of its practices with the STC, such as sending officials to the STC to help establish standard operating procedures and sharing various initiatives, such as a visa revocation program. The STC has compiled a list of 40 administrative and operational best practices throughout the South Texas region for the potential application of the practices region-wide. The STC has implemented two of the identified best practices, an OAM fuel-saving program that provides bulk fuel prices for marine vessels and a physical training regimen to improve the daily duty performance of employees, and as of April 2014, according to STC officials, was also in the process of implementing an auto parts concession program.[14] However, this list of best practices compiled by the STC has not been shared with other CBP collaborative mechanisms, as CBP has not assessed the extent to which best practices could be identified and shared among the mechanisms.

JFC and STC officials identified opportunities for the sharing of best practices across the various mechanisms. For example, an official at one STC component we interviewed noted that the STC should encourage additional sharing of best practices and that components should seek them out for continued growth. However, a senior STC official was unaware of efforts to apply STC best practices outside of the South Texas region. CBP headquarters officials stated that the STC planners used some informal lessons learned from the JFC when planning the STC and noted that the STC benefitted from the JFC having been established first. Sharing of practices, however, has not been ongoing. JFC officials stated that some JFC practices, such as the coordinated process of prioritizing and managing air assets, should serve as best practices for potential replication in other parts of the country, but that CBP has not made a systematic effort to share these practices, although the JFC has shared some practices on an ad hoc basis. An assessment of the JFC and STC mechanisms could help provide CBP with insights on areas for possible improvement and best practices that could be shared among the mechanisms.

In addition to resource management challenges and limited sharing of best practices across the mechanisms, CBP officials we interviewed identified concerns regarding the structure and operations of the JFC. Specifically, senior Border Patrol officials in Arizona told us that, in their view, the JFC has added an unnecessary layer to CBP operations in the state and that it was unclear to them what added capabilities the mechanism was providing. Border Patrol headquarters officials stated that, in their view, CBP should evaluate the JFC to determine whether

---

[14]The Auto Parts Concession program establishes on-site, independently operated auto parts concession stores to support CBP fleet operations. For example, prior to the establishment of concessions stores, sectors ordered parts in bulk. This required excessive storage space and isolated costs in a single fiscal year. Now, parts ordering and payment are conducted online and parts are delivered the same or next day to the repair location. The STC reports more efficient fleet operation, better accountability of vehicle maintenance, and cost savings and avoidance as successes of the concession stores.

changes are needed to the way the mechanism is structured and operated. These officials suggested that changes could be made to the JFC, such as letting POEs maintain responsibility for their daily operations and focusing more on targeted enforcement instead of focusing primarily on the allocation and control of CBP resources.

JFC officials noted that the establishment of the JFC was a major realignment of CBP operations in Arizona as well as a cultural change for personnel in the field. The officials noted that field-level resistance to the JFC is not unexpected given the massive undertaking of the realignment, and that the components are now recognizing the benefits of the JFC. However, an assessment of the JFC and STC could help position CBP to evaluate the effects of these mechanisms, best practices that could be shared among the mechanisms, and any areas for possible improvement, such as management of resources. Senior JOD officials stated that the JOD could help to ensure that JFC and STC local operational objectives are in line with nationwide objectives and make sure that the objectives are being met for more consistent nationwide monitoring. These officials stated that since the JOD is a new organization that is developing and being shaped by CBP, it has not assessed CBP's collaborative mechanisms, including reviewing the potential sharing of best practices. These officials stated that CBP at the agency level needs to decide which mechanisms are working and to fund them based on an informed analysis. However, no entity within CBP has been directed to complete an assessment.

CBP and its components have taken some steps to assess the JFC and STC; however, these actions have not been completed and do not evaluate the effects of these mechanisms, best practices that could be shared among the mechanisms, and any areas for possible improvement, such as management of resources. First, CBP initiated a review of the costs and benefits of the JFC. CBP's Office of Administration (OA) began work on the cost-benefit analysis of the JFC in April 2013 in response to direction in the explanatory statement accompanying the fiscal year 2013 DHS Appropriations Act.[15] According to CBP officials, a draft cost-benefit analysis was completed in September 2013 and provided to the CBP Commissioner's office for review; however, as of April 2014, the analysis

---

[15]Explanatory Statement, Consolidated and Further Continuing Appropriations Act, 2013, 159 Cong. Rec. S1287, S1550 (daily ed. Mar. 11, 2013).

has not been approved by the Commissioner and CBP officials could not provide us with a time frame for when the analysis would be approved. CBP OA officials stated that the draft cost-benefit analysis has no findings or recommendations. According to these officials, the draft analysis describes the costs, which are primarily personnel related, and discusses the qualitative benefits of the JFC related to its stated objectives; however, the draft analysis does not address resources needed to maintain the JFC going forward, nor does it evaluate the results achieved through the JFC. Further, according to OA officials, there is no consensus among CBP officials regarding the purpose of the analysis or how it will be used.

In addition to this CBP-wide cost-benefit analysis of the JFC, OFO is conducting its own internal assessment of the benefits and challenges associated with OFO's involvement in collaborative mechanisms, such as the JFC and STC. Senior OFO officials stated that they are conducting this assessment to better understand the various collaborative mechanism structures as well as to determine how OFO is integrated into each mechanism and what resources it is contributing to the mechanisms. The officials said that they anticipate presenting the final assessment to the OFO Assistant Commissioner by July 2014. According to the officials, this assessment by OFO will focus on that component's inputs to the JFC and STC, but is not intended to address other CBP components' input and benefits from participation in those mechanisms.

Although CBP and OFO have taken steps toward assessing the JFC and STC, these assessments are not intended to provide CBP with information to evaluate challenges across components participating in these mechanisms or determine ways to address those challenges. Best practices for interagency collaboration call for federal agencies engaged in collaborative efforts to create the means to monitor and evaluate their efforts to enable them to identify areas for improvement.[16] Further, according to these best practices, reporting on these activities can help key decision makers within the agencies, as well as clients and stakeholders, to obtain feedback for improving both policy and operational effectiveness. Best practices also indicate that collaborating agencies

---

[16]GAO-06-15.

should identify the human, information, technology, physical, and financial resources needed to initiate or sustain their collaborative effort.[17]

In September 2013, we reported that collecting and assessing information on existing collaborative mechanisms would enable DHS to better monitor these mechanisms.[18] In December 2010, we also reported that DHS could benefit from an assessment of operations along the northern border to identify outstanding challenges and develop planned corrective actions.[19] Specifically, we found that officials in the field were left to resolve coordination challenges without adequate headquarters involvement. While CBP's current efforts to assess the JFC and STC are limited, or focus on a single component, an assessment of the JFC and STC could help CBP better determine the effects of these mechanisms, best practices that could be shared among the mechanisms, and any areas for possible improvement, such as management of resources. CBP's memo to the Secretary of Homeland Security establishing the JFC in February 2011 notes that Arizona will be the site of CBP's first JFC structure, suggesting that CBP may seek to establish additional JFC structures in other geographic areas. Senior CBP officials explained that CBP may look to expand these mechanisms; however, CBP has not finalized the cost-benefit analysis and has not made efforts to evaluate the STC. An assessment could help inform CBP decision making regarding any future uses or changes to the collaborative mechanisms.

DHS Could Strengthen Coordination by Establishing Written Agreements and a Monitoring Mechanism

ACTT and STC Unified Command partners reported positive aspects of coordination; however, officials from 11 of 12 partner agencies we contacted reported coordination challenges.[20] Officials we interviewed from CBP headquarters and the partner agencies reported benefits of coordination, including increased information sharing and improved

---

[17]GAO-12-1022.

[18]GAO-13-734.

[19]GAO, *Border Security: Enhanced DHS Oversight and Assessment of Interagency Coordination Is Needed for the Northern Border,* GAO-11-97 (Washington, D.C.: Dec.17, 2010).

[20]In this section of the report, we provide the results of interviews with ACTT and STC Unified Command partners, including the number of partners of each mechanism that identified a specific area as a coordination challenge, such as limited resource commitments by participating agencies. The other ACTT and STC Unified Command partners did not identify these areas as challenges during the interviews.

planning for joint operations. For example, CBP headquarters officials and partners noted that intelligence sharing among agencies has improved because of the establishment of the ACTT and STC Unified Command. However, our discussions with officials from ACTT and the STC Unified Command partner agencies identified three barriers that they most frequently stated hindered effective coordination within their mechanisms: (1) limited resource commitments by participating agencies, (2) lack of common objectives, and (3) limited outreach to interagency partners.[21] Written agreements and a strategic-level monitoring mechanism could better position DHS to address these challenges and strengthen coordination among partner agencies participating in the ACTT and STC Unified Command.

Limited resource commitments by participating agencies. Our interviews with officials from ACTT and STC Unified Command partner agencies identified challenges associated with limited partner resource commitments to the collaborative mechanisms. As stated in the ACTT charter, the ACTT is intended to engage individual agencies through a joint and cooperative effort to maximize resources toward a common strategy; however, officials from three of six ACTT partner agencies we interviewed cited resource challenges as a barrier to effective coordination. For example, a partner with the ACTT noted that resources are limited for all partners, and that there have been operations in which partners did not follow through with the resources they had committed during the planning stages. Specifically, this official explained how his agency was responsible for leading an overnight operation, which involved the commitment of other ACTT partners. However, the official said that other ACTT partners decided to cover a portion of the overnight operation, rather than the entire operation, without communicating the change in resources to the lead agency or the ACTT, a decision that shortened the length of the operation. Also, another ACTT partner stated that an operation was hampered by lack of resources from an interagency partner. In this case, the ACTT partner said that his agency was unable to apprehend a group of illegal entrants because it did not have the authority

---

[21]Similar coordination challenges were raised in an internal DHS assessment of the ACTT by the Homeland Security Advisory Council in the fall of 2011. Per the request of the former secretary of homeland security, the ACTT was assessed by the Homeland Security Advisory Council Southwest Border Security Task Force. See Homeland Security Advisory Council, *Southwest Border Task Force Report: Third Set of Recommendations* (Washington, D.C.: Fall 2011).

to detain or arrest the entrants, and the agency did not have resources from an interagency partner with those authorities. The ACTT partner stated that it would be helpful to establish a partnership agreement regarding the level of resources that agencies can commit to joint operations.

Additionally, according to ACTT officials, the ACTT has experienced challenges finding interagency partners to contribute personnel to the ACTT staff. Border Patrol, ICE, the Arizona Department of Public Safety, and the Arizona National Guard are the four entities that provide staff to the ACTT. While the ACTT Charter states that the ACTT staff is to be recruited by individual agencies, there is no agreement among ACTT partners regarding how many staff will be provided or by which partners. Members of the ACTT staff said that, in their view, a number of different interagency partners should have the opportunity to lead the ACTT to better reflect a whole-of-government effort, in which partners participate jointly, as noted in the ACTT Charter; however, they stated that no agencies other than CBP and ICE have expressed an interest in assuming a leadership role in the ACTT.

Further, the STC Campaign Plan reflects the intention of the STC Unified Command to take a whole-of-government approach, with partner agencies contributing resources to enhance operations; however, officials from five of six STC Unified Command partners we interviewed cited resource challenges as a barrier to effective coordination. For example, an STC Unified Command partner stated that it can be difficult to address specific targets, such as a "stash house," which is a property that a criminal network may use to harbor illegal entrants, because of not having a sufficient resource commitment from investigative agencies. This partner stated that the success of the STC's Unified Command is predicated on a whole-of-government approach in which all partner agencies provide ample resources. Another STC Unified Command partner stated that agencies may be reluctant to share personnel with the STC Unified Command because of pressure within these agencies to dedicate resources strictly for internal agency initiatives, rather than multiagency efforts.

Lack of common objectives. Our interviews with officials from ACTT and STC Unified Command partner agencies identified lack of common objectives as a barrier to coordination, which could result in limited sharing of information between interagency partners. Officials from three of six ACTT partner agencies and four of six STC Unified Command partner agencies cited lack of common objectives as a challenge.

Specifically, according to officials from some of these partner agencies, as CBP is a lead agency of the ACTT and the STC, those mechanisms have been more focused on helping CBP achieve its interdiction objectives, rather than the missions of the various interagency partners. For example, one ACTT partner stated that the ACTT has not taken the priorities of investigative agencies into account when planning joint operations, which has marginalized these agencies. This partner noted that in some instances valuable operations have collapsed prior to implementation because ACTT partners could not reach consensus regarding whether and how to proceed because of the ACTT's focus on interdictions. An STC Unified Command partner also noted that, in his view, the STC Unified Command has been more focused on interdictions, which has resulted in inadequate information sharing between CBP and investigative agencies, such as ICE and the Drug Enforcement Administration. In addition, DHS and CBP headquarters officials stated that the lack of common objectives between CBP and investigative agencies has been an ongoing challenge and has resulted in limited information sharing between the agencies.

Limited outreach to interagency partners. Our interviews with officials from ACTT and STC Unified Command partner agencies identified challenges associated with limited outreach from the mechanisms to interagency partners. Specifically, officials from two of six ACTT partner agencies cited limited outreach as a barrier to coordination. One partner stated that the ACTT has not provided partner agencies with a sufficient understanding of how the ACTT is different from other multiagency task forces and initiatives in Arizona, in his view contributing to less support for the mechanism among interagency partners. Another partner noted that the ACTT has not communicated its approach to prioritizing resources across the focus areas, which has created a lack of alignment between the focus areas. Moreover, officials from four of six STC Unified Command partner agencies we interviewed noted that STC leadership could improve its outreach to federal, state, and local entities in order to increase awareness of how the STC Unified Command can serve different partners' needs. For example, one partner stated that the STC Unified Command has incorporated one of the partner agency's locations in South Texas into the STC Unified Command; however, the STC Unified Command has not conducted outreach to the agency's other locations in the area. Consequently, the official stated that these other locations either do not know about the STC Unified Command or are not yet aware of the value that the mechanism can provide. This partner noted that gaining the support of all area offices is important in helping the STC Unified Command to build cases against criminal networks as opposed to making individual apprehensions without knowledge of the broader threat environment. Senior STC headquarters officials noted that the STC Unified Command can do a better job of conducting outreach to interagency partners.

Establishing ACTT- and STC Unified Command-specific agreements with interagency partners could help better position DHS to address these challenges. While there are broader agreements in place between some federal agencies relating to agency authorities, protocols, and responsibilities along the southwest border, ACTT- and STC Unified Command-specific partnership agreements have not been developed or implemented. Best practices for interagency collaboration call for the development of written agreements to document collaboration.[22] These practices indicate that as agencies bring diverse cultures to the collaborative effort, it is important to address these differences to enable a cohesive working relationship and to create the mutual trust required to enhance and sustain the collaborative effort. Written agreements, in part, provide a legal framework to improve partnerships, facilitate information exchange, define tasks to be accomplished by each entity, and establish written assurances of each entity's commitments.

Accordingly, we have previously recommended that collaborations would benefit from a formal written agreement. For example, in April 2013, we recommended that DHS examine the potential benefits of written agreements between Border Patrol and tribes to address border security coordination issues.[23] We concluded that written agreements could help DHS and tribal governments come together as partners to establish complementary goals and strategies for achieving shared results in securing the border on tribal lands. Moreover, in March 2006, in response to a GAO recommendation, DHS, the U.S. Department of the Interior (DOI), and the U.S. Department of Agriculture (USDA) signed a memorandum of understanding (MOU) related to border security efforts

---

[22]GAO-06-15 and GAO-12-1022.

[23]GAO, *Border Security: Partnership Agreements and Enhanced Oversight Could Strengthen Coordination of Efforts on Indian Reservations*, GAO-13-352 (Washington, D.C.: Apr. 5, 2013).

on federal lands.[24] The agreement defines the resource commitments of each agency related to areas such as operations and training, outlines common goals, and specifies outreach activities designed to enhance communication among the parties. In November 2010 we found that DHS, DOI, and USDA could better implement some provisions of the agreement; however, we concluded that information sharing among the parties increased since establishment of the MOU.[25]

Officials from CBP noted that ACTT- and STC Unified Command-specific partnership agreements do not exist because there is a tendency to depend on informal relationships among partner agencies and there may be some concern about making a written commitment, which would hold agencies accountable for multiagency efforts in addition to their internal agency initiatives. However, written agreements could serve as a guiding document or overarching statement of principles for ACTT and STC Unified Command participants, including specifying the types and levels of participation and resources by agencies, delineating common objectives, and defining outreach activities to enhance awareness across agencies. For example, the ACTT Chief of Staff stated that the ACTT is facing coordination challenges, such as lack of common objectives, and noted that a partnership agreement could help document partner resource commitments and achieve higher-level buy-in to ACTT objectives and missions. According to this official, establishment of such a written agreement would need to be initiated at a higher level, such as by DHS, since many partners are components within larger organizations. Senior Border Patrol officials in South Texas stated that the STC Unified Command would also benefit from an overarching written agreement, or agreements, with partner agencies, which could serve as a road map among the agencies and could help delineate resource commitments.

In addition, establishing a monitoring mechanism could help better position DHS to address challenges and strengthen coordination among DHS components and components from other federal, state, and local

---

[24]Department of Homeland Security, Department of the Interior, and Department of Agriculture, *Memorandum of Understanding Regarding Cooperative National Security and Counterterrorism Efforts on Federal Lands along the United States' Border* (Washington, D.C.: March 2006).

[25]GAO, *Border Security: Additional Actions Needed to Better Ensure a Coordinated Federal Response to Illegal Activity on Federal Lands*, GAO-11-177 (Washington, D.C.: Nov. 18, 2010).

agencies that participate in the ACTT and STC Unified Command. There is no DHS headquarters-level monitoring mechanism for coordination among DHS components participating in the ACTT and the STC Unified Command, or the external coordination efforts of the ACTT or the STC Unified Command. However, such a mechanism could help DHS, at a strategic level, to monitor the implementation of any written agreements to address the coordination challenges we identified, particularly related to agencies' resource commitments to the ACTT and STC Unified Command and establishment of common objectives. For example, as previously discussed, officials from ACTT and STC Unified Command partner agencies we interviewed identified challenges associated with limited partner resource commitments to the collaborative mechanisms. Written agreements could help document partner resource commitments to the ACTT and STC Unified Command, and a DHS-level monitoring mechanism could help the department monitor implementation of resource commitments identified in the written agreements. Moreover, as previously discussed, officials from some ACTT and STC Unified Command partner agencies we interviewed cited challenges related to lack of common objectives. As the ACTT and STC Unified Command are led by DHS component agencies, a DHS strategic-level monitoring mechanism could help support and review the establishment of common objectives among partner agencies and help better ensure that those common objectives are appropriately balanced among the missions of interagency partners.

Officials from both the ACTT and STC have also said that a DHS-level monitoring mechanism could strengthen these collaborative mechanisms. For example, ACTT staff members noted that DHS is not involved with the ACTT and stated that more DHS headquarters involvement is needed to monitor the whole-of-government effort and to create a unified strategy. The ACTT Chief of Staff suggested that increased DHS engagement at the strategic level could improve coordination among DHS component partners, help better integrate ACTT partners, and serve as an example for other partners to increase their participation. Moreover, senior STC headquarters officials stated that operations in the field are evolving more quickly than operations at the headquarters level, and the success of collaborative mechanisms is predicated on headquarters-level monitoring. Further, the Executive Director of the JOD stated that a DHS-level mechanism to monitor the ACTT and STC Unified Command would help in ensuring that these mechanisms are operating in a strategic manner.

In addition, an assessment of DHS's collaborative mechanisms by the Homeland Security Advisory Council found that DHS's collaborative mechanisms would benefit from strategic-level monitoring at the headquarters level.[26] Specifically, this assessment found that headquarters-level support could help to set and monitor specific objectives for the mechanisms and improve outreach to interagency partners, among other things. Further, in documentation establishing another border security collaborative mechanism, DHS identified the importance of a DHS headquarters leadership entity or monitoring mechanism. For example, the charter establishing DHS's ACTT in New Mexico and West Texas stated that a leadership group at the DHS headquarters level would be beneficial in providing guidance to collaborative mechanisms, and should be composed of senior officials from each DHS component.

In September 2013, we reported that DHS's limited visibility over the universe of collaborative field mechanisms operating under its purview reduced its ability to maximize the effectiveness and efficiency of these mechanisms to enhance cross-departmental management and integrated operations.[27] Specifically, DHS senior officials stated at the time that the components, not the department, are responsible for the mechanisms' oversight because the department is more focused on strategic rather than operational-level management activities. In addition, a DHS senior policy official during our review indicated that a monitoring mechanism at the DHS headquarters level would be beneficial if it functions in a strategic manner, rather than managing the operations of collaborative mechanisms. Standards for Internal Control in the Federal Government indicates that controls should generally be designed to ensure that ongoing monitoring occurs in the course of normal operations and assesses the quality of performance over time.[28] Such monitoring should be performed continually and ingrained in the agency's operations. Further, best practices for interagency collaboration state that federal agencies can enhance and sustain collaborative efforts by, in part, developing mechanisms to monitor and evaluate their results to identify areas for improvement.[29] These practices indicate that monitoring can be achieved through various means, such as establishing a leadership

---

[26]See Homeland Security Advisory Council, Southwest Border Task Force Report: Third Set of Recommendations (Washington, D.C.: Fall 2011).

[27]GAO-13-734.

[28]GAO/AIMD-00-21.3.1.

[29]GAO-06-15.

council to oversee coordination efforts or conducting regular progress reviews.

DHS could benefit from strategic-level monitoring of the ACTT and the STC Unified Command, as the department is accountable for the resources that support these mechanisms and ensuring that components, such as CBP and ICE, are integrated. In addition, DHS is better positioned than the components to increase collaboration and resolve potential issues with other departments participating in collaborative mechanisms, such as the Department of Justice. Specifically, a DHS-level monitoring mechanism could help address the coordination challenge that the ACTT and the STC Unified Command are facing related to lack of common objectives across agencies. A department-level monitoring mechanism could also help better position DHS to ensure that DHS agencies participating in the ACTT and the STC Unified Command are following provisions established in any written agreements, including resource commitments.

Conclusions

Security threats along the southwest border highlight the importance of integrated operations and interagency coordination with respect to DHS's border security efforts. DHS has established collaborative mechanisms in Arizona and South Texas to help better integrate CBP components and facilitate coordination with federal, state, local, tribal, and military homeland security partners. These mechanisms have coordinated CBP and interagency partner efforts through areas such as information sharing, resource targeting and prioritization, and leveraging of assets.

DHS and CBP have established processes to report on the results of the JFC, ACTT, and STC. Although these reporting processes are in place, opportunities exist for CBP to more thoroughly address integration and coordination challenges. For example, CBP has not completed an assessment of the benefits and challenges of the JFC and STC. An assessment looking across the JFC and STC could help CBP evaluate the effects of these mechanisms, best practices that could be shared among the mechanisms, and any areas for possible improvement, such as management of resources. Moreover, while interagency partners report benefits of participation in these collaborative mechanisms, participants we interviewed identified barriers to effective coordination, including limited partner resource commitments and lack of common objectives. Written agreements specific to ACTT and STC Unified Command participation could provide a mechanism to help resolve coordination issues, such as resource commitments. Further, DHS does not have a headquarters-level monitoring mechanism to oversee the interagency coordination efforts of the ACTT or STC Unified Command. A monitoring mechanism could help address ACTT and STC Unified Command coordination challenges related to lack of common objectives, resolve potential issues among interagency partners, and help ensure that partner agencies are following parameters established in partnership agreements, including resource commitments. Establishing written agreements and a monitoring mechanism could be helpful in minimizing ongoing coordination issues related to the ACTT and the STC Unified Command and help DHS to develop more effective collaborative field mechanisms.

Recommendations for Executive Action

To strengthen coordination within the JFC and STC, we recommend that the Commissioner of CBP complete an assessment of the JFC and STC, including evaluating the effects of these mechanisms, best practices that could be shared among the mechanisms, and any areas for possible improvement, such as management of resources.

To strengthen coordination among partner agencies participating in the ACTT and the STC Unified Command, we recommend that the Secretary of Homeland Security take the following two actions:

1. establish written agreements with interagency partners participating in the ACTT and the STC Unified Command, and

2. establish a strategic-level mechanism to monitor the interagency coordination efforts of the ACTT and the STC Unified Command.

Agency Comments and Our Evaluation

We provided a draft of this report to the Departments of Defense, Homeland Security, the Interior, and Justice for review and comment. The Departments of Defense, the Interior, and Justice did not provide comments on our draft report. DHS provided written comments, which are summarized below and reproduced in full in appendix III, and technical comments, which we incorporated as appropriate. DHS concurred with the three recommendations in the report and described actions underway or planned to address them.

With regard to the first recommendation, that CBP complete an assessment of the JFC and STC, DHS concurred and stated that CBP's Joint Operations Directorate will develop a plan to conduct an assessment of the JFC and STC, including the criteria to be evaluated, a timeline for the assessment, and courses of action to conduct the assessment. DHS stated that, based on the plan, the CBP Commissioner will designate an entity to conduct the assessment. With regard to the second recommendation, that DHS establish written agreements with interagency partners participating in the ACTT and the STC Unified Command, DHS concurred and stated that the department will establish a process to develop MOUs for coordination mechanisms along the southern border, including the ACTT and STC Unified Command. DHS noted that it has already taken initial steps in addressing this recommendation, such as creating a strategic framework to guide development of a campaign plan for the southern border. DHS stated that, once completed, this plan will, among other things, include approaches for improved information sharing and inform related efforts, including the development of MOUs with federal, state, local, and international governments. With regard to the third recommendation, that DHS establish a strategic-level mechanism to monitor the interagency coordination efforts of the ACTT and the STC Unified Command, DHS concurred and stated that the DHS Office of Operations Coordination and Planning, in coordination with other components, will establish a strategic-level mechanism to monitor the interagency coordination efforts of the ACTT and STC Unified Command. DHS noted that it has initiated steps toward addressing this recommendation, such as creating the strategic framework to guide development of a campaign plan for the southern border. DHS stated that this plan, once completed, will promote further development of mechanisms for enhanced strategic-level monitoring and interagency coordination. If fully implemented, these and other actions noted in DHS's written comments should help address the intent of the recommendations.

We are sending copies of this report to the Secretary of Homeland Security, appropriate congressional committees, and other interested parties. In addition, this report is available at no charge on the GAO website at http://www.gao.gov.

If you or your staff have any questions about this report, please contact me at (202) 512-8777 or gamblerr@gao.gov. Contact points for our Offices of Congressional Relations and Public Affairs may be found on the last page of this report. Key contributors to this report are listed in appendix IV.

Rebecca Gambler
Director,
Homeland Security and Justice

Appendix I: Objectives, Scope, and Methodology

This report (1) describes how the Department of Homeland Security (DHS) uses collaborative mechanisms in Arizona and South Texas to coordinate border security efforts, and (2) examines the extent to which DHS has established performance measures and reporting processes and how, if at all, DHS has assessed and monitored the effectiveness of the collaborative mechanisms in Arizona and South Texas.

To address these objectives we visited the Joint Field Command (JFC) and the Alliance to Combat Transnational Threats (ACTT) in Arizona and the South Texas Campaign (STC) in South Texas and conducted interviews with officials in U.S. Customs and Border Protection (CBP) headquarters. In Arizona, we visited JFC and ACTT headquarters in Tucson and observed the JFC's Joint Intelligence and Operations Center and an ACTT leadership meeting. We also conducted interviews with JFC and ACTT headquarters officials. In South Texas, we visited STC headquarters in Laredo, where we observed operations at Border Patrol checkpoints and ports of entry (POE) as well as the South Texas Border Intelligence Center, and conducted interviews with STC headquarters officials. During our site visits to Arizona and South Texas, we also met with officials from the Office of Field Operations (OFO), Border Patrol, and the Office of Air and Marine (OAM). Additionally, we conducted semistructured interviews via telephone with CBP component officials in Arizona and South Texas. We selected nonprobability samples of 5 CBP component locations from the 21 CBP component locations in Arizona and 5 CBP component locations from the 43 CBP component locations in the South Texas region. Concerning the JFC, we conducted interviews with officials from the Yuma and Casa Grande Border Patrol stations, the Nogales and San Luis POEs, and the Tucson Air Branch. Regarding the STC, we conducted interviews with officials from the McAllen and Laredo South Border Patrol stations, the Brownsville and Eagle Pass POEs, and the McAllen Air Branch. We selected these JFC and STC component locations based on (1) the type of component (Border Patrol station, OFO POE, or OAM air branch), (2) the level of threat as defined by the number of CBP apprehensions of illegal entrants, and (3) geographic location.

Further, we conducted semistructured interviews via telephone with officials from interagency partners participating in the ACTT and the STC Unified Command. We selected nonprobability samples of 6 ACTT partners from the 66 ACTT partners in Arizona and 6 STC Unified Command partners from the 33 STC Unified Command partners in South Texas. With respect to the ACTT, we interviewed officials from the U.S. Immigration and Customs Enforcement (ICE), National Park Service, Arizona National Guard, Arizona Department of Public Safety, Sierra

Vista Police Department, and Tohono O'odham Police Department.
Regarding the STC Unified Command, we interviewed officials from the
CBP Rio Grande Valley Border Patrol station; CBP Laredo Field Office;
Drug Enforcement Administration (Houston); ICE (San Antonio); Bureau
of Alcohol, Tobacco, Firearms and Explosives (San Antonio); and the
U.S. Assistant Attorney's Office (Laredo). We selected these agencies
based on a range of factors, including (1) type of governmental unit
(federal, state/county, local, tribal, or military), and (2) the level of
participation in the mechanism as defined by leadership role. While we
cannot generalize information obtained from these interviews to all CBP
component offices and intergovernmental partners in Arizona and South
Texas, we selected these locations and partners to provide examples of
the way CBP has integrated and coordinated border security efforts. We
used the results of semistructured interviews with CBP component offices
in the field and interagency partners to identify the primary areas of
integration and coordination of the collaborative mechanisms.

To describe how the Department of Homeland Security (DHS) uses
collaborative mechanisms in Arizona and South Texas to coordinate
border security efforts, we reviewed program documentation and
interviewed officials from CBP. Specifically, we reviewed documents
obtained from JFC, ACTT, and STC officials covering the time frame
2009 through 2014, such as charter documents, establishment memos,
and organizational charts, to identify the structure and roles and
responsibilities for each mechanism. We also reviewed campaign and
operational plans, as well as performance reports, to determine
coordination efforts of the mechanisms. Further, we interviewed CBP
headquarters officials, including officials from the Office of Administration
(OA) and the Joint Operations Directorate (JOD), regarding DHS's
coordination efforts in Arizona and South Texas.

To examine the extent to which DHS has established performance
measures and reporting processes and how, if at all, DHS has assessed
and monitored the effectiveness of the collaborative mechanisms in
Arizona and South Texas, we analyzed campaign plans, after-action
reports, and accomplishment reports from 2011 through 2014 obtained
from the collaborative mechanisms to determine what measures are in
place to track program results and outcomes. In addition, we conducted
interviews with officials from Border Patrol, OFO, and OAM headquarters
to determine the extent to which CBP and its components are assessing
the benefits and challenges of the JFC, ACTT, and STC. We used our
interviews with CBP's JOD and OA to determine the extent to which CBP
is evaluating the JFC and STC mechanisms to identify challenges and

potential best practices for replication. Additionally, we reviewed partnership agreements in place among interagency partners in Arizona and South Texas, as well as a previous DHS assessment of collaborative mechanisms in the field.[1] We evaluated CBP's integration and coordination efforts against best practices for implementing interagency collaboration.[2] We also compared CBP's monitoring efforts against criteria in the *Standards for Internal Control in the Federal Government*.[3]

We conducted this performance audit from June 2013 to June 2014 in accordance with generally accepted government auditing standards. Those standards require that we plan and perform the audit to obtain sufficient, appropriate evidence to provide a reasonable basis for our findings and conclusions based on our audit objectives. We believe that the evidence obtained provides a reasonable basis for our findings and conclusions based on our audit objectives.

---

[1]Homeland Security Advisory Council, *Southwest Border Task Force Report: Third Set of Recommendations*, (Washington D.C.: Fall 2011). Per the request of the former secretary of homeland security, the ACTT was assessed by the Homeland Security Advisory Council (HSAC) Southwest Border Security Task Force as part of a larger study on the potential for expanding the corridor security concept throughout the southwest border environment.

[2]GAO, *Results-Oriented Government: Practices That Can Help Enhance and Sustain Collaboration among Federal Agencies*, GAO-06-15 (Washington, D.C.: Oct. 21, 2005); GAO, *Managing for Results: Key Considerations for Implementing Interagency Collaborative Mechanisms*, GAO-12-1022 (Washington, D.C.: Sept. 27, 2012); and *Standards for Internal Control in the Federal Government*, GAO/AIMD-00-21.3.1 (Washington, D.C.: Nov. 1, 1999). We developed effective practices to enhance and sustain interagency collaboration in GAO-06-15 and GAO-12-1022 by interviewing experts in the area of collaboration and gathering information on select areas where federal agencies have developed substantial ongoing collaborations. These practices are applicable to collaborative mechanisms DHS has established along the southwest border in Arizona and South Texas, as these mechanisms involve interagency collaboration and are intended to help strengthen coordination of border security efforts among participating agencies.

[3]GAO/AIMD-00-21.3.1.

Appendix II: List of Partners in the Alliance to Combat Transnational Threats and South Texas Campaign Unified Command

Alliance to Combat Transnational Threats	U.S. Border Patrol Tucson and Yuma Sectors
	U.S. Customs and Border Protection Office of Field Operations
	U.S. Immigration and Customs Enforcement Homeland Security Investigations (HSI)
	U.S. Immigration and Customs Enforcement Enforcement and Removal Operations (ERO)
	Drug Enforcement Administration (DEA)
	U.S. Attorney's Office
	U.S. Department of the Interior
	Bureau of Alcohol, Tobacco, Firearms and Explosives (ATF)
	U.S. Department of Agriculture
	Bureau of Land Management
	U.S. Forest Service
	U.S. Fish and Wildlife Service
	U.S. Citizenship and Immigration Services (USCIS)
	U.S. Marshals Service
	U.S. Secret Service
	Transportation Security Administration (TSA)
	U.S. Department of State
	National Park Service
	Arizona Department of Public Safety
	Arizona High Intensity Drug Trafficking Areas
	Tucson Counter Narcotics Alliance

State of Arizona Attorney General

Pima County Attorney

Santa Cruz County Attorney

Maricopa County Attorney

Yuma County Attorney

Pinal County Attorney

Cochise County Attorney

Pima County Sheriff

Santa Cruz County Sheriff

Maricopa County Sheriff

Yuma County Sheriff

Pinal County Sheriff

Cochise County Sheriff

Graham County Sheriff

Gila River Police Department

Tohono O'odham Police Department

Ak-Chin Indian Community Police Department

Phoenix Police Department

Tucson Police Department

Nogales Police Department

Patagonia Police Department

Sahuartia Police Department

South Tucson Police Department

Marana Police Department

Oro Valley Police Department

Casa Grande Police Department

Eloy Police Department

Maricopa Police Department

San Luis Police Department

Yuma Police Department

Wellton Police Department

Benson Police Department

Bisbee Police Department

Douglas Police Department

Huachuca City Police Department

Safford Police Department

Sierra Vista Police Department

Tombstone Marshal's Office

Willcox Police Department

Thatcher Police Department

Arizona National Guard

Arizona Joint Counter Narco-Terrorism Task Force

Luke Air Force Base

U.S. Army Criminal Investigation Command Fort Huachuca

South Texas Campaign Unified Command

Laredo Border Patrol Sector Chief Patrol Agent

Del Rio Border Patrol Sector Chief Patrol Agent

Rio Grande Valley Border Patrol Sector Chief Patrol Agent

New Orleans Border Patrol Sector Chief Patrol Agent

Laredo Field Office Director of Field Operations

Houston Field Office Director of Field Operations

Southwest Region Director

San Antonio Federal Bureau of Investigation Special Agent in Charge

Houston DEA Special Agent in Charge

San Antonio HSI Special Agent in Charge

Houston HSI Special Agent in Charge

Southern District of Texas U.S. Marshal

Laredo DEA Assistant Special Agent in Charge

San Antonio DEA Assistant Special Agent in Charge

McAllen DEA Assistant Special Agent in Charge

Dallas DEA Assistant Special Agent in Charge

San Antonio ATF Resident Agent in Charge

Houston ATF Special Agent in Charge

Corpus Christi U.S. Coast Guard Captain

Joint Task Force North Lieutenant Colonel

U.S. Army North Colonel

San Antonio USCIS District Director

San Antonio USCIS Records Manager

San Antonio ERO Field Office Director

Houston ERO Field Office Director

Laredo Assistant U.S. Attorney

CBP Internal Affairs Special Agent in Charge

CBP Assistant Chief Counsel

CBP Attaché Mexico City

TSA Field Security Director

Texas Department of Public Safety Regional Director

South Texas High Intensity Drug Trafficking Area Director

Houston High Intensity Drug Trafficking Area Director

U.S. Department of Homeland Security
Washington, DC 20528

Homeland
Security

June 9, 2014

Rebecca Gambler
Director, Homeland Security and Justice Issues
U.S. Government Accountability Office
441 G Street, NW
Washington, DC 20548

Re: Draft Report GAO 14-494, "BORDER SECURITY: Opportunities Exist to Strengthen
       Collaborative Mechanisms along the Southwest Border"

Dear Ms. Gambler:

Thank you for the opportunity to review and comment on this draft report. The U.S. Department of
Homeland Security (DHS) appreciates the U.S. Government Accountability Office's (GAO) work in
conducting its review and issuing this report.

The Department is pleased to note GAO's recognition of U.S. Customs and Border Protection (CBP)
efforts of utilizing a whole of government approach to secure geographic corridors. By employing a
collaborative enforcement approach, leveraging the capabilities and resources of DHS agencies in
partnership with other federal state, local and tribal partners, CBP strives to increase its operational
effectiveness to better disrupt, dismantle and ultimately defeat transnational threats that are
exploiting the border region.

Two leading examples of these efforts illustrated in GAO's report are the Joint Field Command
(JFC) in Arizona and the South Texas Campaign (STC) in South Texas. In addition, CBP led the
effort in 2009 to launch the Alliance to Combat Transnational Threats (ACTT); a collaborative
enforcement effort that leverages the capabilities and resources of more than 60 federal, state, local,
and tribal agencies in Arizona and the Government of Mexico to combat individuals and criminal
organizations posing a threat to communities on both sides of the border.

The draft report contained three recommendations with which the Department concurs. Specifically,
GAO recommended that the CBP Commissioner:

Recommendation 1: Complete an assessment of the JFC and STC, including evaluating the effects
of these mechanisms, best practices that could be shared among the mechanisms, and any areas for
possible improvement, such as management resources.

Response: Concur. As an office within the Office of the Commissioner, CBP's Joint Operations
Directorate will develop a plan to conduct an assessment of the JFC and STC. This plan will be
submitted to the Commissioner, and will establish the criteria to be evaluated, a timeline which

identifies an assessment period and other pertinent milestones, and courses of action to conduct the assessment. The Commissioner will designate the entity responsible for the assessment and initiate the assessment period. Estimated Completion Date (ECD): To Be Determined (TBD).

GAO also recommended that the Secretary of Homeland Security:

Recommendation 2: Establish written agreements with interagency partners participating in the ACTT and the STC Unified Command.

Response: Concur. The DHS Office of Policy (PLCY) in coordination with the DHS Office of Operations Coordination and Planning (OPS), CBP, and other Components, as appropriate, will develop a process by which memoranda of understanding (MOUs) will be developed in order to better facilitate partnerships in support of Southern Border coordination mechanisms, including the ACTT and STC Unified Command. The Department has already taken initial steps toward addressing this recommendation, beginning with the recent creation of a DHS-wide U.S. Southern Border and Approaches Strategic Guidance/Framework, intended to guide development of a DHS-wide Southern Border and Approaches Base Campaign Plan. Once completed (on or before September 30, 2014), this plan will include approaches for improved information sharing, sensor integration, and unified command and control structures, as appropriate, and inform related efforts and processes including the development of MOUs with Federal, state, local, and international governments. Development of an MOU process will begin within one year following completion of the Campaign Plan. ECD: TBD.

Recommendation 3: Establish a strategic-level mechanism to monitor the interagency coordination efforts of the ACTT and the STC Unified Command.

Response: Concur. Various branches within OPS, in coordination with PLCY, CBP, and other Components, as appropriate, will establish a strategic-level mechanism to monitor the interagency coordination efforts of the ACTT and STC Unified Command. The Department has already initiated significant steps toward addressing this recommendation, beginning with the recent creation of a DHS-wide U.S. Southern Border and Approaches Strategic Guidance/Framework to guide development of a DHS-wide Southern Border and Approaches Campaign Plan. Once completed on or before September 30, 2014, this plan will promote further development of mechanisms and new processes for enhanced strategic-level monitoring through situational awareness, and interagency coordination on a broader level, to include ACTT and STC Unified Command operations. Development of these mechanisms will begin within one year following completion of the Campaign Plan. ECD: TBD.

Again, thank you for the opportunity to review and comment on this draft report. Technical comments were previously provided under separate cover. Please feel free to contact me if you have any questions. We look forward to working with you in the future.

Sincerely,

Jim H. Crumpacker, CIA, CFE
Director
Departmental GAO-OIG Liaison Office

2

Appendix IV: GAO Contact and Staff Acknowledgments

GAO Contact	Rebecca Gambler, (202) 512-8777 or GamblerR@gao.gov
Staff Acknowledgments	In addition to the contact named above, Jeanette Espínola (Assistant Director), David Alexander, Molly Callaghan, Frances Cook, Joseph Cruz, Anthony Fernandez, Eric Hauswirth, Lauren Membreno, and Jessica Orr made key contributions to the report.

GAO's Mission	The Government Accountability Office, the audit, evaluation, and investigative arm of Congress, exists to support Congress in meeting its constitutional responsibilities and to help improve the performance and accountability of the federal government for the American people. GAO examines the use of public funds; evaluates federal programs and policies; and provides analyses, recommendations, and other assistance to help Congress make informed oversight, policy, and funding decisions. GAO's commitment to good government is reflected in its core values of accountability, integrity, and reliability.
Obtaining Copies of GAO Reports and Testimony	The fastest and easiest way to obtain copies of GAO documents at no cost is through GAO's website (http://www.gao.gov). Each weekday afternoon, GAO posts on its website newly released reports, testimony, and correspondence. To have GAO e-mail you a list of newly posted products, go to http://www.gao.gov and select "E-mail Updates."
Order by Phone	The price of each GAO publication reflects GAO's actual cost of production and distribution and depends on the number of pages in the publication and whether the publication is printed in color or black and white. Pricing and ordering information is posted on GAO's website, http://www.gao.gov/ordering.htm. Place orders by calling (202) 512-6000, toll free (866) 801-7077, or TDD (202) 512-2537. Orders may be paid for using American Express, Discover Card, MasterCard, Visa, check, or money order. Call for additional information.
Connect with GAO	Connect with GAO on Facebook, Flickr, Twitter, and YouTube. Subscribe to our RSS Feeds or E-mail Updates. Listen to our Podcasts. Visit GAO on the web at www.gao.gov.
To Report Fraud, Waste, and Abuse in Federal Programs	Contact: Website: http://www.gao.gov/fraudnet/fraudnet.htm E-mail: fraudnet@gao.gov Automated answering system: (800) 424-5454 or (202) 512-7470
Congressional Relations	Katherine Siggerud, Managing Director, siggerudk@gao.gov, (202) 512-4400, U.S. Government Accountability Office, 441 G Street NW, Room 7125, Washington, DC 20548
Public Affairs	Chuck Young, Managing Director, youngc1@gao.gov, (202) 512-4800 U.S. Government Accountability Office, 441 G Street NW, Room 7149 Washington, DC 20548